Bygone Days in the Peak District

**Lindsey Porter
and Dudley Fowkes**

BYGONE DAYS
IN THE PEAK DISTRICT

Moorland Publishing

British Library Cataloguing in
Publication Data

Porter, Lindsey
    Bygone days in the Peak District.
    1. Peak, Eng. - Social life and customs -
Pictorial works
    I. Title   II. Fowkes, Dudley Vincent
942.5′11′0810222   DA670.D43

For Pat, Amanda and Andrew

ᶜ   L. Porter and D.V. Fowkes 1979

Reprinted 1986

ISBN 086190 016 2 (paperback)

Printed in Great Britain by :
Dotesios (Printers) Ltd,
Bradford-on-Avon, Wilts
for the publishers:
Moorland Publishing Co Ltd,
8 Station Street, Ashbourne,
Derbyshire, DE6 1DE

Contents

Acknowledgements

Introduction

Life on the Land 1

Minerals and Industry 13

Water 27

Travel by Road 41

Travel by Rail and Canal 62

Street Scenes and
Village Life 85

Halls and Churches 112

Leisure and Recreation 118

Index

Introduction

Nostalgia for the past has grown immensely in the last few years. Perhaps it owes its popularity to the fact that the extent of the changes that this century has witnessed are beginning to make themselves more apparent. Time for leisure pursuits has grown and is still growing, giving one a greater opportunity to study the past. As a measure of the times in which we live, a speaker in a recent House of Lords debate seriously stated that an influencing factor in the desire of many to investigate the past was the TV programme 'Roots'. Whatever the reason, all students of history will agree that our way of life has fundamentally changed from that of our grandparents.

In this book, these changes are illustrated against the backcloth of the Peak District, an area of great physical contrasts and an area which has undergone very variable degrees of change. In terms of landscape, thickly-wooded dales contrast vividly with the bleak limestone plateau, while peripheral market towns, often predominantly brick, which grew up in the area of interchange between highland and lowland, differ markedly from tiny limestone villages on the moorland tops. In terms of degree of change, some sleepy villages that have changed little in their physical appearance for centuries contrast dramatically with areas which the demands of modern society for water and minerals have altered beyond recognition.

The Peak District is surrounded by industrial conurbations and has been the centre of attention, particularly since Victorian times, for people from these areas seeking recreation and the benefits of clean and fresh air. The build up of pressure from tourists, and indeed from commuters, has caused many changes, although the impact of tourism in the area dates back much further as the late eighteenth century development of Buxton and Matlock Baths as spas demonstrates. In more recent years, the whole function of many villages has changed as they increasingly perform the role of dormitories for Sheffield and Manchester. As this new function has come to the fore, formerly important local industries such as cotton spinning and weaving, metal working industries such as needle-making and, of course, lead mining have declined or disappeared completely.

The pressure from tourists and commuters has been more than matched in recent years by the apparently insatiable appetite of modern society for minerals found in the area and for one of life's basic needs, water. The Peak has paid a heavy price for being an upland area of high rainfall surrounded by large centres of population, as large tracts of land, including whole communities, have vanished beneath a network of reservoirs begun in the middle of the last century. This continues right through to the present day as we await the first moves to form the new Carsington Reservoir. Due to the vigilance of local photographers, the stages in the inundation of the upland valleys has been

faithfully recorded and we are fortunately able to show a selection of their work in this volume. Of particular note are the photographs of Birchinlee, Derbyshire's long-forgotten 'shanty town'.

Over the last hundred years quarrying has changed dramatically from a small scale industry serving basically local needs with relatively little effect on the landscape, to an activity conducted on a massive scale, by international companies with a correspondingly massive impact on the landscape. Derbyshire man beavered away in his lead mines for centuries to produce a characteristic landscape of small humps and hillocks, but nowadays vast areas of the surface can be removed in short periods of time. ICI's quarry at Great Rocks Dale boasting the largest quarry face in Europe. This book features several illustrations of the quarrying industry before the vast changes of scale took place.

Change is not limited to these more extreme examples of course. Other photographs picked for this book bring out some of the gentler aspects of change particularly well. For instance, there are several village street scenes where the only significant change has been the tarmacing of the road and the addition of modern street furniture. Similarly on many of the farms in the area, the changes have been mainly technological. Gone are the days when water was fetched from the well in a water barrel or in buckets suspended from a yoke; no longer do farmers drive their animals to market; but the basis of the farm economy, the farm buildings and the general pattern of farm life remain much the same. Modern forms of entertainment, television and radio in particular have of course, brought about further great changes in our way of life, in the Peak District as elsewhere. The photographs from Ashbourne in particular demonstrate how our ancestors were willing to celebrate any local or national event at the drop of a hat by turning out in the streets, dressing up and performing in pageants and the like, and thus providing much of the community entertainment of the day.

Back to the more dramatic changes, transportation systems have seen many changes in the area over the last 100 years and not just because of the internal combustion-engine, although that has undoubtedly had the most far-reaching effects. Not only has the horse and cart been made obsolete but also many of the area's railways and all of its trams (oh yes, the Peak District had them prior to the National Tramway Museum being established at Crich!). In many ways the railways have come and gone as far as large parts of the Peak are concerned, as the series of photographs of the main Matlock-Buxton line and the Cromford and High Peak Railway remind us. Undoubtedly, because of the popularity of the theme as a subject for photography, this book could have been filled with only railways photographs, so just a representative few have been selected to keep the balance of the book.

Photographs are important, giving a visual impression of how life has changed. Relatively few of those reproduced here are the work of professional photographers or even of historians deliberately setting out to record events; many of them in fact came to light, as so often is the case, in cupboards, chests-of-drawers or other odd corners, among private papers and odds and ends. If you find some which you wish to dispose of or are willing to have copies made, show them to your local library or record office.

Source of Photographs:

C.L.M. Porter Collection: 1-3, 5-7, 12-13, 15-16, 19, 29, 41-45, 47, 49-52, 59-60, 72-73, 77, 89-91, 99-101, 105-107, 109-112, 115, 117, 120-121, 127, 132, 135-136
D.V.Fowkes Collection: 95-98, 104, 123
W.W. Green Collection: 4, 10, 11, 20, 30-32, 53, 62-63, 102, 116, 124
Derbyshire Record Office:
    D1035: 8-9, 33-40
    D1589: 22-24, 27-28, 71, 103
    Strutt Collection: 17, 48, 69-70, 92, 94, 97
    1397B/B17: 54
    1799M/Z15-16: 57-58
    1799M/236: 93
    1397B/B145: 122
    18882/23: 125
    Brooke-Taylor Collection: 21
    Thornhill Collection: 25
    D1485: 79
H.M. Parker Collection: 14, 26
British Rail: 46, 65
J. Ellis: 55-6
Ramblers' Association (Manchester Branch): 133
A.J.M. Henstock Collection: 61, 75-76, 85-88, 118-119, 128-131
Knighton Collection: 64, 66-68
Derbyshire Life: 74
Locomotive and General Railway Photographs: 80-83
Rev G. Prime: 108
M. Swales: 113
P. Wilson: 114
D. Berwick: 134
Waterways Museum, Stoke Bruerne: 78
E. Paget-Tomlinson: 84

Life on the Land

1

One of the main industries of the Peak District is agriculture. Farming has been an important element of the economy since man first populated the area. These photographs portray some of the activities of the farmer, both on the land and on market day.

1   In some ways village life has changed a great deal, take this view of a farmer walking a pig for instance!

2   The Horsefair at Leek. This autumn fair was also a hiring fair where farm labourers hoped to gain labour for the forthcoming year. Here the photographer has recorded a group of gipsies selling a horse in the old Smithfield Market. The number of bowler hatted gentlemen is interesting; they were probably the local gentry or their agents at the fair to hire labour and purchase livestock.

3 Droving animals to market. Droving was a common practice before cattle trucks enabled animals to be moved quickly and efficiently. Here cattle are approaching the Parish Church at Leek.

4

5

4 Regular visitors to the Hope Valley will still recognise this view of Hope Church, but are now unlikely to find a sheep and cattle fair being held on the main street as it still was in the early years of this century. The importance of sheep in the Derbyshire economy tends to be overlooked and relatively little has been written about it.

5 Market day in Leek: a scene typical of many Peak towns like Bakewell, Buxton, Ashbourne and Wirksworth. Wares are spread out beneath the covered stalls much the same as today, although hens, geese, etc, have now disappeared from the scene. The Red Lion Hotel on the right was a coaching inn and dates from the seventeenth century. Leek is fortunate in that its cobbled market place is still cobbled although unfortunately the remaining cobbled streets have recently been covered with tarmac.

6 Purchasing a fowl at Leek Market some 75 years ago. Street traders such as this man have largely disappeared except for the covered market stalls. How smart the purchaser appears in her outfit and straw hat.

7 Hygiene regulations would prevent this from happening today. Here cheeses are stocked on the pavement in the Market Place at Leek. They were possibly Derby Cheeses from the cheese factory at Reapsmoor near Longnor.

8 Cattle grazing around the village pond at Wetton in the early 1940s. The village watering place was a characteristic feature of many Peakland villages. In the days before piped water they were obviously of great importance but in recent years some have fallen into disuse and some, including this one, have even disappeared. Cattle, like sheep, were an important element in the Peak District economy from prehistoric times, being kept both for milk — converted into cheese in the days before modern forms of transport — and beef. Cheese making was less important in the Peak than in the lower-lying lusher pastures to the south.

9 Horse-drawn plough at work at an unspecified location in the Peak District, probably during the war years (1939-45). Although livestock farming has always dominated the area, for obvious reasons most of the villages outside of the moorland areas had sufficient arable land to fulfil their own needs.

10 Another familiar sight in the traditional Peakland scene — sheep shearing at Howden House, close to Howden Reservoir, and dating from the turn of the century. Sheep farming gave rise to the earliest textile industries of the High Peak area, a domestic woollen industry long preceding the cotton industry for which the area became famous. Sheep were traditionally the basis of farming in the High Peak, going back to prehistoric times when the Neolithic (or New Stone Age) farmers first introduced them.

11 The sheepwash at Birchinlee Bridge, Derwent Woodlands, in the early years of this century, just before the construction of the Howden and Derwent Reservoirs which flooded large areas of the Derwent Valley.

12 Now completely obsolete, the domestic yoke once had a vital function in daily life when water and milk had to be fetched and carried. Seen in Longnor about his daily business is Mr George Tunnicliffe.

Minerals and Industry

Apart from farming, minerals have given rise to the Peak's earliest industries, lead being mined from the Roman period, and stone being quarried for as long as man has inhabited the area. There were, of course, other industries using the natural resources of the area such as paint works, brick works, etc, but in the main they have all now disappeared.

13   Here we have a study of a brick maker at work. Brickworks occurred around the Peak District serving local needs, all having succumbed to economic depression. Some areas had a wealth of them. Leek had three in one street alone. George Smith ran one at Reapsmoor near Longnor from about 1850. He later became an MP for Coalville in Leicestershire and championed the cause of children employed in brickworks as well as on canals etc. While at Reapsmoor he refused to employ either child or female labour.

14   Millclose Mine at Wensley, was Britain's richest lead mine, producing from 1861 to 1939 ore worth over £20 million. By the 1930s daily production was 800 tons of crude ore; seven million gallons of water a day had to be pumped from 900ft below ground and over 700 men were employed there. The Old Millclose Mine was reopened in 1859 when the beam engine seen here was erected. The photograph probably dates to before 1874 when the engine stopped working, but it remained there for another twelve years. In this scene there are over forty people, including boys and to the left the mine owner and overseers.

15   This group of miners at Millclose, probably early this century, are seen measuring the lead ore by volume in a wooden 'dish'. This was the traditional method of measuring ore in the Peak.

16

17

Drawn by F.L.Chantrey. A.R.A.

Engraved by W.B.Cooke.

16 Much of the copper ore produced at the Ecton Copper Mine was refined in the Churnet Valley, where the copper works of Thomas Bolton & Sons still survives at Froghall. The firm had a large works at Oakamoor which was demolished in 1963. It was here that the copper core of the first Atlantic Cable was produced in 1856. Here we have a scene in Mill Road, Oakamoor. All the mill buildings shown here date from the mid to late nineteenth century and have now gone.

17 Lead was mined in the Peak District from Roman times and the industry continued to be an important contributor to the local economy until the nineteenth century. In the late seventeenth century the reverberatory furnace was introduced for smelting lead, replacing earlier furnaces and the primitive hearths or 'boles' of the medieval period, and lead smelting 'cupolas' were scattered on elevated sites throughout the upland area. The Alport Cupola shown here was developed by the Barker family in the early nineteenth century.

18 Another long-standing lead-smelting site is Middleton Dale, the twisting limestone gorge at Stoney Middleton. Nowadays it is a busy centre of the quarrying industry but as Sir Francis Chantrey's 1818 engraving shows it was once characterised by the chimneys of the furnaces as well as numerous limekilns.

19 The main mine on the ore field which did not primarily produce lead was Ecton Copper Mine in the Manifold Valley. After repeated attempts at reworking the mine in the nineteenth century one last attempt was made in 1883 by Ecton Co Ltd. Here miners are grouped together at the entrance to Clayton mine when the level was being rerailed in 1883-4. Note the miner's special hat; it is a Bradder Beaver and these were manufactured at Bradwell near to Castleton.

21 One such larger quarry to develop this century is the Stancliffe gritstone quarry at Darley Dale. This view shows the quarry in operation in about 1920 with a steam crane being used to lift the massive blocks of stone. The quarry had its own private railway and note that the small saddle-tank pictured is named *Sir Joseph* after Sir Joseph Whitworth, the engineer and philanthropist who lived at nearby Stancliffe Hall. Massive increases in demand from the building industry, road and railway construction and industry in general have caused a revolution in scale in the quarrying industry.

20 A Foster steam tractor belonging to Hadfields of Hope hauling roadstone from Pindale Quarry to Hope Station in 1912. Before the modern massive requirements of stone for roads and ballast for railways, small quarries were set aside in most Peakland villages for stone for repairing the roads.

22 A mid nineteenth-century photograph of Bottoms Mill, Longdendale, on the River Etherow. This mill disappeared when much of Longdendale was flooded for Manchester Corporation Waterworks between 1866 and 1881. The Peak District became an important area for the early factory cotton spinning industry when water power was the key locating factor. Fast flowing streams in remote upland valleys were characteristic sites for cotton mills in the late eighteenth century before

23

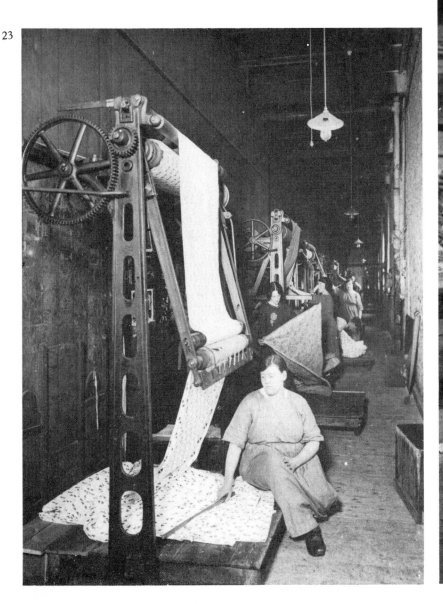

steam-powered mills became the rule. Cotton mills were frequently built on the site of early corn mills or, occasionally, lead mills.

23/24 Two views of mill-hands at work on calico printing machinery at Dinting Vale Printworks in the 1920s. In the first photograph cloth is emerging from the hot-air drying chambers after printing. Note that the woman is wearing clogs. The operatives in the second photograph are working on plaiting or folding machines. Dinting Vale Works, near Glossop, was an outlier of the Lancashire-based calico printing industry. The works was originally a typical small upland cotton mill, built in 1817 by Joseph Lyne of Simmondley Hall. It was converted to calico-printing by Edmund Potter and his brother Charles in 1825. Potter was later to become the world's largest calico printer.

25 The burnt-out shell of Sir Richard Arkwright's cotton mill at Bakewell after it had been destroyed by fire in 1868. Bakewell was the second of Arkwright's water-powered cotton spinning mills in the Peak District, being built six years after Cromford in 1777 on land leased from Philip Gell. The base of the structure was later incorporated in the D. and P. (Dujardin-Plante) Battery Works which occupied the site from 1897.

26 One of the traditional craft industries of the Peak District was the famous rope-making industry of Castleton which was located in the unlikely setting of the entrance to Peak Cavern, perhaps the most renowned of the area's natural features. This remarkable activity continued on a small scale until the recent retirement of Bert Marrison pictured here.

Water

A further natural resource of the Peak is water. Both the Derwent and Longdendale valleys have a complex of reservoirs and many other areas in and around the national park have been flooded, either for domestic purposes or for feeding the canal system, such as Rudyard Lake near Leek.

27/28 Not all the floods in the Peak District have been intentional. Glossop is not located on a major river, but these two photographs show what can happen when the small fast-flowing streams that powered the cotton mills burst their banks after heavy rain in 1941.

29 This large weir in the Dane Valley below Wincle impounded water to provide a supply for a feeder channel to Rudyard Lake. The trout ladders provided the means to restore fishing to the upper reaches but these have gone now, along with the original footbridge which collapsed. The weir presumably dates from around 1800 when Rudyard Lake was being built.

30 While minerals and manufacturing industry remain of great importance, one of the Peak District's major exports this century has been water. The construction of the three Derwent reservoirs since 1900 has had a major impact on the landscape and not only in terms of the creation of the lakes themselves. This photograph shows the main street of Birchinlee, the temporary settlement built to house the workers on the construction of the Howden and Derwent Reservoirs between 1901 and 1916. This photograph dates from about 1905 and the sweet shop in the right foreground was run by the Bateman family.

31 Pay day at Howden for construction workers on the Howden and Derwent Dams, about 1905.

TOWN HALL & MARKET SQUARE,
DERWENT VALLEY WATER WORKS.

32 Another view of Birchinlee village street in about 1905 showing the mobile butcher's shop in the 'Market Square', with the white-painted 'Town Hall' in the left of the picture. The site of Birchinlee is now a plantation.

33

33 The construction of Howden and Derwent Reservoirs, opened in 1912 and 1916 respectively, was followed by the construction between 1935 and 1945 of the larger Ladybower Reservoir, also by the Derwent Valley Water Board. Unlike Howden and Derwent, the flooding of the Derwent Valley for Ladybower involved the destruction of two hamlets, Ashopton and Derwent, and the closure and diversion of several roads. This photograph shows the Ashopton Inn, one of the major casualties in Ashopton.

34

34 The demolition of the Ashopton Inn.

35 Ashopton Village before the flood,
showing the main street and the
Ashopton Inn.

36 A scene in Derwent village.

37/38 Ladybower Reservoir in the course of construction, showing the construction of the concrete piers of the bridge carrying the new road across the Derwent Valley at Ashopton. The construction of the Ladybower Dam involved the building of a 1,250ft embankment, 140ft high, using 100,000 tons of concrete, 100,000 tons of clay and one million tons of earth in the process.

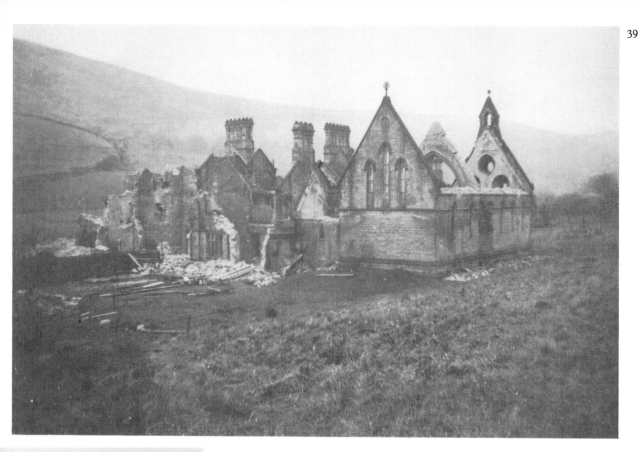

39 Derwent Hall in the process of demolition.

40 Derwent Hall and grounds after demolition with Derwent Church still standing.

Travel by Road

41 Returning from the market, the farmer and his horse seem to show well the feeling that these were more leisurely days, although it must have been a chilly ride in the wintry weather. Taken at Thorncliffe near Leek, about 1900.

42/43 Horse-drawn transportation was indispensable prior to the internal combustion engine. An interesting feature in the 1890s was the stage coach run from Alton Towers to Buxton via Leek. The coach *Greyhound* was often driven by the Earl of Shrewsbury himself and left Alton Towers at 10.00am to Leek via Threelowes. The 25 miles to St Annes Hotel, Buxton, was covered in 3½ hours. The return trip left Buxton at 3.00pm and returned to Alton via Cheadle, the return fare being 15s (75p). Presumably, the trips were made periodically during the summer months when the earl was at the Towers. These two views show the coach at Alton Towers and leaving the Market Place, Leek.

44

46 A now-busy trunk road in less hectic times — the A6 just outside Bakewell on the way to Ashford in about 1900. This photograph is of railway origin and may have been taken for use in railway carriages.

47 This fine photograph of a carrier was taken in Stockwell Street, Leek in 1903. His sturdy covered cart would be well suited to his occupation and to the rough roads of the district. It is often overlooked that the well known carriers Messrs Thomas Pickford owned the Goytsclough Quarry on Axe Edge, near Buxton, in the seventeenth century.

44 A particularly fine coach and pair at Swythamley Hall, the home of the Brocklehurst family.

45 This unusual scene of a horse drawn sleigh was taken at Hulme End in the Manifold Valley. Note the faithful dog keeping close by.

45

48 Engraving of a stagecoach in
Ashwood Dale on what is now the A6,
just outside Buxton, some time in the
early nineteenth century. At this date
this was part of the Ashford to Buxton
turnpike, created in 1812 to improve
that section of road. The ancient route
through Derbyshire to Manchester was
not through Duffield, Matlock and
Bakewell, but ran some way to the west
through Kedleston, Hognaston and
Brassington and across the moors to
Buxton. The present line of the A6 was
improved by a series of small turnpike
trusts between 1756 and 1815.

49   Here a fine example of a household
carriage is being loaded with provisions
adjacent to the Cock Inn, Derby Street,
Leek. Note the many baskets sitting on
the roof of the carriage and the brake on
the rear wheel. The use of two horses
reflects the need for extra pulling power
in hilly areas. What a clatter the iron-
rimmed wheels must have made upon
the cobbled streets.

50/51 Steam road transport was
perhaps not so common but a Straker
steam bus was a regular feature from
Leek and Ashbourne to Waterhouses
and Buxton to Hulme End to serve the
new Manifold Valley light railway.
Featured here are the bus picking up at
the site of the Monument, Leek and the
bus at Lowe Hill bridge. The buses
used to frighten horses and it was
common to find the driver dismounted
and holding his horse by the bridle.
The buses were in use from 1904.

52 This view of the steam bus at Waterhouses is particularly interesting because it shows the original temporary station built where the Manifold Valley narrow gauge railway crossed the Leek to Ashbourne road. This station served until the standard gauge line arrived later and the permanent station was built nearer the village.

53

53 A group about to leave the Old Hall Hotel, Hope, about 1910 on a charabanc outing. This vehicle belonged to the hotel and could be hired for outings in the Peak District. Reg Hall of Bradwell was the driver.

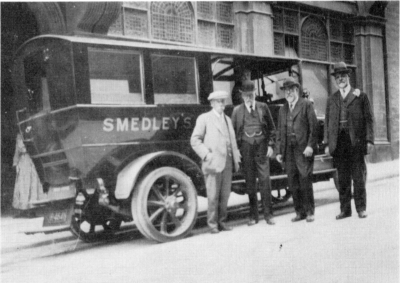

54 An early motor 'bus belonging to Smedleys Hydro at Matlock photographed outside the Hydro some time in the 1920s. No doubt the bus supplemented the cable tramway in ferrying patrons of the Hydro up Matlock Bank. John Smedley first started a hydro on Matlock Bank in 1851 in a house acquired from Ralph Davis of Darley Dale. It was immediately successful and work started on the present building in the late 1850s. Extensions continued to be added until 1890, by which time the popularity of hydropathy had passed its peak.

56 Hartington has always been one of the major tourist centres of the Peak District. Porter's charabancs would have been regular visitors to the village, or on this occasion, to the Charles Cotton Hotel. The name would have been comparatively new at the time the photograph was taken and had previously been known as the Sleigh Arms.

55 The group of Ford Model-Ts drawn up in the Market Place at Hartington is a far cry from today. Note the rough limestone surface to the road, typical of the whole district in pre-tarmac days. Although physically this village scene has altered little, the number of parked vehicles has increased considerably.

57/58 Two views of the Matlock
cable tramway both taken around 1910.
The coming of the hydros to Matlock
brought about the linking of the two
settlements of Matlock Bank and
Matlock Bridge, and the opening of the
cable tramway in 1893 very much
cemented this union, providing
transport up Matlock Bank from
Crown Square to Wellington Street just
beyond Smedley's Hydro. The first
photograph shows the tramway
terminus in Crown Square now
removed to nearly Hall Leys Park, and
the second a tram on its journey down
Matlock Bank with the Town Hall on
the left. Decline in interest in the
hydros and an accompanying general
decline in Matlock as a tourist centre
led to the closure of the tramway in
1929.

57

59 An essential part of the communication system before the telephone was the telegraph boy, delivering his telegram on his bicycle or horse. Here, he is delivering a telegram at Butterton, by the ford.

60 The Leek Cyclists' Club is one of the oldest cycling clubs in the country being founded in 1876. This photograph shows the club on one of its weekend runs complete with penny farthing bicycles. Note the smaller bike for the young lad.

61 The widening of Hanging Bridge, Mayfield, near Ashbourne, in about 1927. Note the length of temporary railway line built for the steam crane. The ancient bridge at Hanging Bridge is mentioned in Quarter Sessions records as far back as 1671 and can still be seen beneath the more recent arches.

Travel by Rail and Canal

62 *French* — named after the Boer War general — at the Derwent Valley Water Board's siding at Bamford in about 1910. This small locomotive was used from 1902 to 1913 at Derwent Reservoir hauling excavated material from the reservoir site.

63 The timber viaduct at Ashopton carrying the Derwent Valley Water Board's private railway across the Derwent in about 1904. The viaduct was built by Messrs Scott and Middleton, the contractors for the railway. This line was a temporary affair providing materials for the construction of the reservoirs.

64 It is hard to imagine nowadays that this large group of late Victorian passengers are in fact waiting at a small village station, namely Rowsley, on the Midland Railway's line to Buxton. This is not the original Rowsley station, the terminus of the 1849 branch from Ambergate, designed by Paxton, but the later station on the Rowsley and Buxton extension, planned in 1858, but not opened until 1867.

66 Chinley Old Station in the 1890's prior to its demolition and replacement by the much grander station which is still in use. Chinley became an important point of interchange between the London-Manchester line and traffic between Sheffield and the North West following the opening of the Dore and Chinley line in 1894. It is doubtful, however, whether the amount of passenger traffic generated at the junction ever justified the ambitious new Chinley station.

65   Matlock Bath Station 1889,
showing the original extended gable
end which was cut back some time
before 1910, and the signal box in its
pre-1893 position. The line from
Ambergate to Rowsley was opened
under the grandiose title of the
Manchester, Buxton, Matlock and
Midland Junction Railway in 1849. It
was, of course, eventually extended to
Manchester, and it is interesting to note
that it has now contracted to almost its
original length.

68 Stationmaster I'Anson and his
staff at Bakewell in about 1910. How
times have changed! Even in the
context of the greater volume of traffic
in Victorian and Edwardian times, it is
difficult to envisage a station of
Bakewell's modest size with a staff of
eighteen. Had it survived to the present
day, it would now doubtless be an
unstaffed halt!

67 Timber from Oxford received at
Bakwell station for use in the
restoration of Bakewell church roof in
1906. In 1906 all the railway companies
would claim to be able to move
anything anywhere!

69 Construction work in progress on the Cowburn Tunnel on the Dore and Chinley line in about 1890. This line was built as a rival to the Manchester, Sheffield and Lincolnshire Railway's trans-Pennine route via Woodhead and Penistone, and was one of the last parts of the Midland Railway's main line system to be built. Originally a private company was to build the line in 1884 but it gained insufficient support and the Midland took it over.

70 The Chapel Milton viaduct in the Dore and Chinley Railway in the course of construction in about 1890. This viaduct linked a spur of the Dore and Chinley line with the London to Manchester line north of Chapel-en-le-Frith station, enabling trains to run from Sheffield to the quarrying areas around Peak Forest and Buxton without turning.

71 Dinting viaduct on the Manchester, Sheffield and Lincolnshire Railway's Manchester to Sheffield line, the first line to link the two cities, opened as early as 1845. The main line of the railway just by-passed the then expanding cotton town of Glossop and a short branch was built from Dinting at the eastern end of the viaduct to Glossop. The building of a branch was financed by Lord Howard, who owned much of Glossop. He subsequently sold it to the railway company.

72 Rail transport in the Peak District was not extensive owing to the nature of the terrain and the views shown here are from one of the more unusual lines. The Manifold Valley Light Railway was well known and much photographed. The line was opened in 1904 by The Earl of Dartmouth, the Lord Lieutenant of Staffordshire, and the arch shown here was built in his honour at Waterhouses.

73 This is perhaps one of the most well known of all the photographs taken of the Leek and Manifold Valley Light Railway. It shows the train and its primrose-yellow coaches at Hulme End Station shortly after the opening of the line. The unusual design of the locomotives is a result of them being copies of engines built for the Barsi Light Railway in India, although the cow catchers, with which the locomotives were supplied, were never used! The line was a tourist attraction but failed to generate the local trade for which it was built and it closed in March 1934 after only thirty years operation.

74

74 After closure the line remained unused for a while before the rolling stock was brought into use once more for the job of demolishing the line. One of the line's two locomotives, *E.R. Calthrop,* is shown here below Thors Cave Station. Shortly after this, all the rolling stock with a minor exception, was scrapped.

75

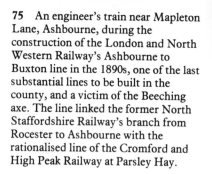

75 An engineer's train near Mapleton Lane, Ashbourne, during the construction of the London and North Western Railway's Ashbourne to Buxton line in the 1890s, one of the last substantial lines to be built in the county, and a victim of the Beeching axe. The line linked the former North Staffordshire Railway's branch from Rocester to Ashbourne with the rationalised line of the Cromford and High Peak Railway at Parsley Hay.

76

76 Ashbourne Station around the turn of the century with a Uttoxeter bound passenger train in the platforms and a minute shunting locomotive in the station yard. The station has now been demolished and replaced by a car park.

77 Canals did not play a great role in the area of the Peak District as they only came to the edges of it. The uplands were crossed by roads and railways only and indeed the Cromford and High Peak Railway was built to connect two canals. In the south, the Caldon Canal served the Churnet Valley and surrounding districts. This scene shows a narrow boat loaded with stone moored at Cheddleton Wharf. The stone is likely to be limestone, loaded at Froghall Wharf, from the Caldon Low Quarries. This scene has changed with the widening of the road and of course, the loss of commercial traffic.

78 The Cromford Canal showing coal wagons waiting to be loaded at Cromford Wharf in 1906. The firm of Wheatcroft and Sons operated at Cromford Wharf as coal merchants throughout the life of the canal and have only recently closed down. At one time they operated a passenger service along the canal from Cromford to Nottingham at single fares of 4s first class, 2s second class. Two years after this photograph the boats would have been able to travel along only 8¼ miles of canal due to the collapse of the Butterley Tunnel in 1908.

79

80

79 One of the first railways in the Peak District was the Cromford and High Peak Railway, planned in 1824, and opened by 1830. This photograph shows the workshops at High Peak Junction at the southern terminus of the line around the turn of the century. The railway was built to link the Cromford Canal near Cromford with the Peak Forest Canal at Whaley Bridge, providing a remarkable water and rail through route from the East Midlands to the North West. A series of stretches of horse-drawn tramway were punctuated by inclined planes on the inevitable steep gradients of this extraordinary upland route. Not surprisingly the route was never successful as a through route as progress was painfully slow even by the standards of the day, but the development of quarries along the route gave the line a long life despite its obvious disadvantages. What a boon the line must have been in an area not noted for easy transportation in early days. The trains even brought water to the upland areas in specially adapted wagons.

80 This very early locomotive was built for the Cromford and High Peak Company at an early date, possibly in 1841. It survived on the line until 1871 when it was transferred to Crewe by the L&NWR who had taken over working of the line. The driver must have felt very exposed in the bleak days of winter on this upland railway.

81/82 The former Cromford and High Peak Railway was noted for its inclines. These two photographs show wagons at the top and bottom respectively of the 1 in 8 to 1 in 9 Sheep Pasture incline. The wagons were hauled up the incline on a cable to which the wagons were attached. Note the catchpit between the rails, visible through the bridge, in order to catch runaway wagons. A broken wagon still remains embedded in the pit.

83 A 'Crewe Goods' tank locomotive No 3049 at the top of the Hopton incline. This was the steepest locomotive-worked incline in use on British Railways when it closed in 1967. The line served chiefly local quarries and factories, rather than the local inhabitants, although passengers were carried for a time.

84 Taken about 1905, this scene is on the Peak Forest Tramway. The construction of the line commenced in 1795 and it survived until 1926, carrying limestone. The whole affair was somewhat crude; note the flangeless wheels on the 'L' shaped rails which were of 3ft length laid on stone blocks. The wagons ran downhill under gravity and were stopped by throwing a hook and chain into the wheels. The high incidence of wheel breakage resulted in wheels being placed along the line and two are visible here.

Street Scenes and Village Life

85 Some of the inhabitants of Church
Street, Ashbourne, gathered around the
neighbourhood pump, celebrating one
of Queen Victoria's Jubilees.

86 The top of Ashbourne Market Place with the market in progress in late-Victorian times. Stalls are conspicuously absent with the tradesmen just using their carts to display their wares. Uncluttered by twentieth century street furniture and motor cars the area looks surprisingly spacious. Compare this with Fig. 5 where the market is more typically crowded.

88 Market Street Ashbourne around 1900 with a coach parked in the foreground. The market stalls on the pavement outside the porticoed Town Hall would now be in the middle of the road, as the road has been considerably widened at this point.

87 The yard of Ashbourne's best known public house, The Green Man, in late Victorian times.

89

90

89 A market scene at Leek, looking through the archway to the former Golden Lion Yard at the rear of the inn of the same name, which formerly existed in Church Street before a road widening scheme resulted in the demolition of all the properties opposite the church. Taken about 75 years ago.

90 Not a sight to be witnessed today, here we have a scene showing a travelling salesman, or 'cheap-jack' as they were known, with his wares set out on the middle of the main road through Leek. His all-male audience seems to be engrossed with his sales patter, except perhaps for the boy to his right who stands in bare feet, head in hands looking rather bored with it all.

91 Everyone likes a good procession and several are depicted in these pages. This shows the annual Club Day in Leek when the Sunday School children and other organisations walk around the town following a Church service in the town's market place. The small boy and girl depicted here await the arrival of the procession and banners, in their best clothes.

92 An early nineteenth-century engraving of the Crescent at Buxton, a tremendous contrast to the vernacular architecture of most of the area's towns. Buxton was developed as a spa by the Romans, but most of the notable buildings in the town centre date from the late eighteenth century when the then Duke of Devonshire, who owned much of the central area of the town, developed it on a grand scale. He commissioned John Carr of York to design many of the buildings including the Crescent. The centre of gravity of the town moved away from the old centre around the Market Place to the area around the Thermal Baths and the Crescent.

Pavilion and Promenade, Buxton

93 Encouraged by the opening of the
railway from Manchester, Buxton
continued to develop as a tourist and
conference centre throughout the
nineteenth century, one result being the
building in 1871 of the Winter Gardens
and Pavilion displayed here in about
1910. Edward Milner was the architect.

94 Landscaping was an essential
element in the new Regency Buxton as
is demonstrated by the 1833 engraving
of 'The New Promenade Walks'.

DRAWN ETCHED & PUBLISHED

THE NEW PROMENADE WALKS

FROM THE POST OFFICE STEPS

BUXTON.

BY H. MOORE. DERBY. 1833

95 A view of the centre of late
Victorian Wirksworth looking down the
Market Place towards North End with
the Town Hall in the foreground. At
this date the only way out of the town to
the north was via North End, as
Harrison Drive, leading in to the
immediate left of this picture, had yet
to be built. The Town Hall was built by
a private company in 1871, and could
house 600 people.

96 A heavily-laden cart parked on St
Johns Street, Wirksworth, around the
turn of the century. Despite a
pedestrian crossing and other modern
street furniture, heavy lorries and
alterations to shop fronts, the view
towards Derby looks much the same
today.

97

98 A quiet scene in Cromford Market Place about 1910 before the erection of railings around the Greyhound Yard.

97 Ashford in the Water about 1895. The main street shown here formed part of the Derby to Manchester road before being bypassed by the present A6. Towards the end of the seventeenth century 300 packhorses with malt from Derby passed through each week. The packhorse bridge with its well-known sheepwash crosses over the River Wye at the end of the street beyond the market stance.

99 Although this particular view in Oakamoor has not physically altered much, it is interesting to see the man collecting water in a water barrel at the village well near the Lord Nelson Inn. The photograph was taken about 75 years ago.

100 Many villages formerly had a lock-up or a set of stocks etc. The circular lock-up at Longnor seen on the right of this photograph has long since vanished but is similar to the one which has survived at Alton. Nearby Warslow has a set of stocks made of iron, and wooden stocks can still be seen at Eyam.

101 A further view in Longnor village, perhaps some 75 years ago, looking towards the Market Place. Note the loading bay from a loft above the shop.

102 A glimpse inside one of the houses at Hope showing the Green family taking tea at the Blacksmith's Cottage, Christmas 1912. Very few Peakland villages were (and still are) fortunate to have a gas supply.

103 The village school became a common feature of the Peakland scene in the last century, as many schools were built between 1840 and 1880, the majority of them church schools. This photograph shows pupils at Tintwistle Church of England School in the late 1890s, taken on the south side of Tintwistle church. The photograph hardly suggests that this was a time of great prosperity in Tintwistle, while the expression on the children's faces hardly suggests that school was much fun either!

103

104 Kirk Ireton main street around the turn of the century. Kirk Ireton was not on the line of a main road and the surface had clearly yet to be made up.

105

105 Hulme End village prior to the tarmac surface to the road being added. The properties on the right appear to be newly built, the stone being unweathered.

106 This group photograph was taken outside The Cock Inn at Upper Elkstones. This small pub has unfortunately closed recently, together with the village shop and school.

107 School girls sliding in the snow outside their school at Middle Hills on the main Buxton to Leek road near the gritstone outcrop known as The Roaches. The school is now a dwelling, having been closed under Staffordshire's plan to close most of their small village schools, but would once have been part of a close-knit community. Most of the girls appear to be wearing clogs.

108 Portrait studies of older generations can often be quite fascinating; fashions change of course and in any-event standards of dress have altered immensely. Here is a local character asleep by the side of the road in Hartington Dale.

109 Mr Pointon the paver with his bowler hat and set-rammer, laying cobbles in a Leek street, probably in the late nineteenth century.

110/111 Here two bearded characters stand in a pub yard with their clay pipes and jugs of ale. Beer was still being served and drunk from standard pint jugs at the Devonshire Arms inn at Sheldon, near Bakewell, until it closed in 1972.

Halls and Churches

Ilam Hall

112 The Peak District has been fortunate in that it has lost very few of its great houses. Perhaps a reason for this is that apart from the outstanding Haddon Hall and Chatsworth House few very large mansions exist. The southern Peak has a small area in which quite a few halls have been demolished partly or completely — for example the halls at Beresford, Throwley, Ilam, Osmaston, Calwich Abbey, Wooton, Snelston, Alton Towers, Ashbourne and Ashenhurst. Here we show Ilam Hall in all its glory.

Banquet Hall, Alton Towers.

113 Alton Towers has long been
popular with tourists and this was so
even when in use as a private house by
the Earls of Shrewsbury, the premier
Earls of England. Although now a
gutted shell it retained much of its
former glory after being sold by the
Talbot family in the 1920s. Here we
have incongrous mass-produced chairs
in the magnificent Banqueting Hall
which had been turned into a cafe.

114 The gardens at Alton Towers
were of special interest when
constructed and really must have been a
beautiful sight. It was here that carpet-
bedding with flowering plants was
supposedly originated on a truly
massive scale. This early photograph of
the gardens gives a hint of the former
splendour, although it must be said that
the gardens are still a credit, even if not
quite so lavish.

115

115 A further hall which now only exists as a gutted shell is Throwley Hall. It had associations with Thomas, Lord Cromwell and Charles Cotton but it was empty and little used in the late nineteenth century. A proposal to turn it into a hotel came to nothing and it is understood that the roof was removed during the World War I. The Tudor stable block remains and is in use as a cowshed. This engraving is dated 1845.

117

117 Demolition of a different kind occurred at Earl Sterndale when the church became a victim of bomb damage from an enemy aircraft during World War II and was gutted by fire. It is interesting that Arthur Goldstraw, the photographer, did not realise that the building was gutted until he developed his film!

116 The major casualty of the formation of Ladybower Reservoir was undoubtedly Derwent Hall, the ancient family seat of the Balguy family. It subsequently belonged to a variety of owners, being described in Lysons' *Magna Britannia* in 1817 as a farmhouse; by any standards rather a large one!

Leisure and Recreation

118 Pageants were another popular feature of Jubilee and Coronation celebrations. The date of this one at Ashbourne is not known, but it seems to feature Britannia, the English king and a variety of foreign adversaries!

118

119 Even in the days of seemingly endless working hours and few holidays Peak District folk had their local customs and sports, perhaps one of the best known being the Ashbourne football game, played largely in the Henmore Brook, between two sides termed the 'Uppards' and 'Downards'. This view shows the match in progress at Back Bridge some time in the 1930s.

120/121   Another widely-known Peak District custom is well dressing, which has gathered momentum in the twentieth century with the great increase in tourism. It has its true origins in pagan customs and in most places its revival is recent. These photographs appropriately show Tissington, perhaps the only place where the custom continued through the centuries. They show Yew Tree Well and The Hall Well around 1900. Only the fashions seem to have changed, the wells being decorated much the same as today.

122   In Matlock, Smedley's Hydro became a great focus for the town's leisure activities between the 1860s and World War II. There were firework displays and banquets, and extensive sporting facilities. This photograph shows a small circus act performing on the lawns in front of the winter gardens in the 1930s.

Wirksworth Cricket Team. Seaso

H. E. Bowmer,   E. Gandy,   C. Pashley,   J. E. Cooke,   A. Killer,   N. P. Wilshi
     W. H. Buxton,   A. Hatfield,   G. H. Bowmer,   Dr. F. M. Seal,   T. Fl

1911.

Hilditch, W. A. Bowmer,

123 Organised sport has really come into its own in the last 120 years or so, and this is as true of the Peak District as any other area. This photograph shows the Wirksworth Cricket Team for the 1911 season. Surely A. Killer must have been a fast bowler!

124 Birchinlee's life was short, but long enough for the village to develop most of the normal village institutions. This shows the village football team in 1912. Judging by the number of trophies and medals in evidence, the club was successful.

125

LOVERS WALKS AND
RIVER DERWENT, MATLOCK BATH.

125 Two aspects of leisure are demonstrated in this 1910 photograph: children providing their own amusement in the form of hoops and a long disappeared 'switchback' in the

River Gardens at Matlock Bath.

126

127 Day trippers to the Cat and Fiddle Inn. Note the stage coach behind the carriage on the left-hand side. This isolated inn is the second highest inn in England and is built on the former turnpike road from Macclesfield to Buxton which itself followed a much older roadway at this point. In 1831 the Cat and Fiddle was described as 'a newly-erected and well accustomed inn'.

126 Buxton and Matlock Bath vied with each other as spa towns and this view of Buxton's Thermal baths is quite interesting. It also shows the Palace Hotel built for visitors to the spa town and the bath chairs available for those unfortunate enough to need the therapeutic properties of the warm thermal waters. A further massive hotel formerly stood near the Palace Hotel (the Empire Hotel) but this was demolished after being empty for many years. Matlock seems to have gone a stage further with such places like the massive Hydro of John Smedley, now the County Offices.

128 Coronations and jubilees have always provided Peakland villages with an excuse for celebrations on a grand scale with fetes, galas, pageants, bazaars, processions and fairs the order of the day. The Ashbourne firemen seem to be taking a leading role in this jubilee gathering in a lavishly decorated Ashbourne Market Place on the occasion of Victoria's Diamond Jubilee in 1897.

129 Another part of the same celebrations is shown here with a decorative arch erected by the town's Sunday Schools.

129

130 This military procession in Church Street Ashbourne, was also part of the 1887 celebrations.

131 St John's Street, Ashbourne, ten years earlier on the occasion of Victoria's Golden Jubilee, is the scene of the street parties shown here.

132 Following closure of the Manifold Light Railway, the line became a public footpath and later the section from Swainsley to Wetton Mill was opened to vehicular traffic. A proposal in 1959 to extend this to Weags Bridge resulted in a protest meeting at Wetton Mill. The scheme was abandoned in the face of stiff opposition from ramblers, conservationists and naturalists.

133 During the early part of this century, demonstrations, protests and mass trespasses occurred by ramblers attempting to gain access to such areas as Kinder Scout, Bleaklow etc. Shown here is the 1928 demonstration in the Winnats Pass near to Castleton. Despite the successful outcome of such rallies as far as Kinder Scout and Bleaklow are concerned, much of the moorland area of the Peak District is still closed and private land, despite being part of a National Park.

134 Today, Grindsbrook, north of
Edale is one of the main routeways up
onto the Kinder plateau and is now the
starting point of the southern end of the
Pennine Way. Before the ramblers
were permitted access, the bleak area of
Kinder was the preserve of the land-
owners and their shooting parties. This
shooting cabin was for their benefit and
was situated in Grindsbrook. The
photograph was taken in 1902.

135 This is a fascinating photograph.
The two ladies are on a rope bridge in
the Dane Valley, and what is more
there appears to be another rope bridge
behind it, with a wooden support
beneath it. The precise location of the
bridge is not certain but it could be
below the trout ladders in Fig 29. Rope
bridges are somewhat rare and no other
is known in the area.

136   Visitors to Dovedale stop at the
site of the stepping stones for
refreshment from the mobile stall.
Presumably the ladies had travelled
down from Thorpe which used to be
very fashionable and they hardly look
kitted out for a walk up Dovedale.
Their refinement would look very
much out of place with the ramblers of
today. Note the horse patiently waiting
by its cart under the dry stone wall.

Index

Alport cupola, 17
Alton, 100
Alton Towers, 42, 113-114
Arkwright, Sir Richard, 25, 97
Ashbourne, 75-76, 85-88, 118-119, 128-131
Ashford in the Water, 97
Ashopton, 33-35, 63

Bakewell, 25, 46, 67-68
Birchinlee, 11, 30, 32, 124
Brick maker, 13
Butterton, 59
Buxton, 48, 92-94, 126

Caldon Canal, 77
Cat & Fiddle Inn, 127
Castleton, 26, 133
Chapel Milton Viaduct, 70
Cheap-jack, 90
Cheddleton Wharf, 77
Chinley Old Station, 66
Coaches, 42-44, 47-49
Cotton Mill, 22, 25
Cowburn Tunnel, 69
Cromford, 97-98
Cromford Canal, 78
Cromford and High Peak Railway, 79-83
Cyclists Club, Leek, 60

Dane Valley, 29, 135
Derwent Hall, 39-40, 116
Derwent reservoirs, 11, 30, 62-63
Dinting Vale Printworks, 23, 24
Dinting viaduct, 71
Dore & Chinley Railway, 69-70
Dovedale, 136
Droving, 3

Earl Sterndale Church, 117
Edale, 134
Ecton Copper Mine, 16, 19
Eyam, 100

Glossop, 23, 24, 27, 28, 71

Hartington, 55-56, 108
Hope, 4, 20, 53, 102
Hopton Incline, 83
Horsefair, 2
Howden, 10, 31
Hulme End, 45, 73, 105

Ilam Hall, 112

Kirk Ireton, 104

Leadmining, 14, 15
Lead smelting, 17, 18
Leek, 2, 3, 5, 6, 7, 43, 47, 49, 89-91
Longdendale, 22
Longnor, 12, 100, 101
Lockup, 100

Manifold Valley Light Railway, 52, 72-74
Matlock, 54, 57-58, 122
Matlock Bath, 65, 125
Mayfield, 61
Middleton Dale, 18
Middle Hills School, 107
Millclose Mine, 14, 15

Oakamoor, 16, 99
Old Characters, 108-111

Pageants, 118
Paver, 109
Peak Forest Tramway, 84
Pindale Quarry, 20
Ploughing, 9
Processions, 91, 130

Railways, 21, 52, 62-76
Rope bridge, 135
Rope making, 26
Rowsley Station, 64

Sheep Pasture Incline, 81-82
Sheep Shearing, 10
Sheep wash, 11
Shrove Tide Football, 119
Smedley's Hydro, 54, 122
Stancliffe Quarry, 21
Steam Bus, 50-52
Swythamley Hall, 44

Thorncliffe, 41
Thors Cave Station, 74
Throwley Hall, 115
Tintwistle, 103
Tissington, 120-121
Tramway, 57, 58

Upper Elkstones, 106

Waterhouses, 52, 72
Well Dressing, 120-121
Wetton, 8

Wetton Mill, 132
Winnats Pass, 133
Winter Gardens, Buxton, 93
Wirksworth, 95-96, 123

Yokes 12, 106